Help Is Here

Finding FRESH STRENGTH and PURPOSE
in the POWER of the HOLY SPIRIT

STUDY GUIDE | FIVE SESSIONS

MAX LUCADO

with ANDREA LUCADO

HarperChristian
Resources

Help Is Here Study Guide
© 2022 by Max Lucado

Requests for information should be addressed to:
HarperChristian Resources, 3900 Sparks Dr. SE, Grand Rapids, Michigan 49546

ISBN 978-0-310-13306-3 (softcover)
ISBN 978-0-310-13307-0 (ebook)

All Scripture quotations, unless otherwise indicated, are taken from the Holy Bible, New International Version®, NIV®. Copyright © 1973, 1978, 1984, 2011 by Biblica, Inc.® Used by permission. All rights reserved worldwide.

Scripture quotations marked NCV taken from the New Century Version®. Copyright © 2005 by Thomas Nelson. Used by permission. All rights reserved.

Scripture quotations marked NKJV taken from the New King James Version®. Copyright © 1982 by Thomas Nelson. Used by permission. All rights reserved.

Scripture quotations marked NLT taken from Holy Bible, New Living Translation, copyright © 1996, 2004, 2015 by Tyndale House Foundation. Used by permission of Tyndale House Publishers, Inc., Carol Stream, Illinois 60188. All rights reserved.

Scripture quotations marked MSG taken from THE MESSAGE. Copyright © 1993, 2002, 2018 by Eugene H. Peterson. Used by permission of NavPress. All rights reserved. Represented by Tyndale House Publishers, a Division of Tyndale House Ministries.

Scripture quotations marked TLB taken from The Living Bible, copyright © 1971 by Tyndale House Foundation. Used by permission of Tyndale House Publishers Inc., Carol Stream, Illinois 60188. All rights reserved. The Living Bible, TLB, and The Living Bible logo are registered trademarks of Tyndale House Publishers.

Any internet addresses (websites, blogs, etc.) and telephone numbers in this study guide are offered as a resource. They are not intended in any way to be or imply an endorsement by HarperChristian Resources, nor does HarperChristian Resources vouch for the content of these sites and numbers for the life of this study guide.

HarperChristian Resources titles may be purchased in bulk for church, business, fundraising, or ministry use. For information, please e-mail ResourceSpecialist@ChurchSource.com.

First Printing July 2022 / Printed in the United States of America

Contents

Note from the Author v

How to Use This Guide vii

Session 1 **Our Powerful Ally** 1

Session 2 **Our Strength and Guide** 21

Session 3 **Our Peace and Guarantee** 41

Session 4 **Our Intercessor and Advocate** 61

Session 5 **Our Gift-Giver of Life** 85

Leader's Guide 105

Note from the Author

I began attending church as a youngster. I was barely into my double-digit years before I was reading my Bible, memorizing Scriptures, and doing my level best to obey every command that I heard preached from the pulpit. I hoisted the backpack of good Christian living and set out to scale the lofty peaks of morality, spirituality, and devotion.

Always tell the truth. Never lag in faith. Pray more. Do more.

Believe me, I tried to tackle that mountain. But that trail grew steep. Peer pressure, raging hormones, and guilt conspired to convince me that I would never make it. Can a fifteen-year-old suffer spiritual burnout? This one did.

Maybe you know the feeling. The fire inside you is running low. It's not for lack of searching. The Lord knows you've tried. At least you *hope* he knows. You've signed up and stood up for everything you know to be right and good. Yet why this cold wind in the face? Why this uphill struggle? These gray skies? This empty spot?

It feels as if life is fading away . . . drip by drip, little by little, day by day.

If that describes what you are feeling right now, the Lord has something—actually, *someone*—you need to know. He is the heaven-sent Helper. The ally of the saint. Your champion, advocate, and guide. He will comfort you and direct you. He will indwell you, transform you, sustain you, and—some-day—deliver you into your heavenly home.

The Bible makes more than a hundred references this *someone* that we know as the Holy Spirit. He is the ultimate teacher (see John 14:26). He is the wind of God (see John 3:8). He is your intercessor (see Romans 8:26). He is the seal of heaven on the saint (see Ephesians 1:13). He is the dove of peace who calms you, the gift-giver who equips you, the river of living water who flows out of you to refresh the world (see John 7:37–39).

In this study, we will ponder the amazing benefit of the divine presence. Whether this is a fresh encounter or your first encounter, it does not matter. God wants you to have the energizing strength of the Holy Spirit. He wants you to know help isn't just coming . . . it is already here. Challenges come with life, but they need not *define* your life. Help is here.

How to Use This Guide

T he Holy Spirit. What comes to mind when you hear that name? If you are like most people, the term itself seems a bit mysterious. God the *Father* is easy enough to grasp. We can comprehend that image. God the *Son* is manageable as well. But God as . . . *Spirit?*

This is the purpose of the *Help Is Here Study Guide.* Over the course of the next five sessions, you will embark on a journey to discover what the Bible says about this third member of the Trinity. You will discover how he can be your ally, your strength, and your guide. You will see that he can give you peace in this world. You will look at his role as your intercessor, your advocate, your giver of spiritual gifts, and—ultimately—your guarantee of eternal life to come.

Now, before you begin, keep in mind that there are few ways you can go through this material. You can experience this study with others in a group (such as a Bible study, Sunday school class, or any other small-group gathering), or you may choose to go through the content on your own. Either way, know that the videos for each session are available for you to view at any time by following the instructions provided on the inside cover of this study guide.

Group Study

Each of the sessions are divided into two parts: (1) a group study section, and (2) a personal study section. The group study section is intended to provide a basic framework on how to open your time together, get the most out of the video content, and discuss the key ideas together that were presented in the teaching. Each session includes the following:

- **Welcome:** A brief introduction to the topic for you to read on your own.
- **Share:** A few ice-breaker questions to get you and your group members thinking about the topic and interacting with each other.
- **Read:** A key passage for you and your group members to read through together before you watch the video teaching.
- **Watch:** Six key points from the video teaching to help you follow along, stay engaged, and take notes.
- **Discuss:** Six questions to help you and your group members reflect more on the material presented in the teaching and apply it to your lives.
- **Respond:** A short personal exercise to help reinforce the key ideas.
- **Pray:** A place for you to record prayer requests and praises for the week.

If you are doing this study in a group, make sure you have your own copy of the study guide so you can write down your thoughts, responses, and reflections and have access to the videos via streaming. You may also want to have a copy of the

Help Is Here book, as reading it alongside the curriculum will provide you with deeper insights. See the "recommended reading" section at the end of each session for the chapters in the book that correspond to the material you and your group are discussing. Finally, keep these points in mind:

- **Facilitation:** If you are doing this study in a group, you will likely want to appoint someone to serve as a facilitator. This person will be responsible for starting the video and keeping track of time during discussions and activities. If *you* have been chosen for this role, there are some resources in the back of this guide that can help you lead your group through the study.

- **Faithfulness:** Your small group is a place where tremendous growth can happen as you reflect on the Bible, ask questions, and learn what God is doing in other people's lives. For this reason, be fully committed and attend each session so you can build trust and rapport with the other members.

- **Friendship:** The goal of any small group is to serve as a place where people can share, learn about God, and build friendships. So seek to make your group a "safe place." Be honest about your thoughts and feelings . . . but also to listen carefully to everyone else's thoughts, feelings, and opinions. Keep anything personal that your group members share in confidence so that you can create a community where people can heal, be challenged, and grow spiritually.

If you are going through this study on your own, read the opening Welcome section and then reflect on the questions that follow in the Share section. Go through the Read section and record your responses in the space provided. Watch the video and use the prompts to take notes. Finally, personalize the questions and exercises in the Discuss and Respond sections and record your thoughts. Close by recording any requests you want to pray about during the week.

Personal Study

As the name implies, the personal study section is for you to work through on your own during the upcoming week. Each exercise is designed to take you deeper into passages of Scripture so that you can further explore the ways, wonders, and workings of the Holy Spirit in your life. Go at your own pace, doing a little each day or all at once, and spend a few moments in silence to listen to what the Holy Spirit might be saying to you. Each personal study will include the following:

- **Opening:** A brief introduction to lead you into the personal study.
- **Scripture:** A few passages on the Holy Spirit for you to read and review.
- **Reflection:** Questions for you to answer related to the passages you just read.
- **Prayer:** A short prayer that you make your own and pray back to God.

Note that if you are doing this study as part of a group, and you are unable to finish (or even start) these personal studies for the week, you should still attend the group time. Be assured that you are still wanted and welcome even if you don't have your "homework" done. The group studies and personal studies are both intended to help you hear what God wants you to hear and how to apply what he is saying to your life. So . . . as you go through this study, be listening for him to speak to you as learn about the Holy Spirit and know that his *help is here*.

Our Powerful Ally

*Paul traveled through Turkey and arrived in
Ephesus, where he found several disciples. "Did you
receive the Holy Spirit when you believed?" he asked
them. "No," they replied, "we don't know what
you mean. What is the Holy Spirit?"*

ACTS 19:1–2 TLB

10min'

Welcome

We could all use a little help sometimes. Perhaps this is why two of the Beatles' catchiest hits included lyrics like, "*I get by with a little help from my friends,*" and, "*I need somebody, help! Not just anybody, help!*"

That last part is very true. Sometimes when we need help, we don't need it from just anybody. We need supernatural help. We need big things to happen. We need a person in our lives to change. We need our own hearts to change. We need the type of help that a fellow human cannot really provide and the type of help that we can't muster on our own.

Enter the *Holy Spirit.*

Now, Christians have all sorts of opinions and reactions when it comes to the Holy Spirit. Some nod their heads and say, "amen." They deeply believe in the power of the Spirit and have witnessed it in their lives. Some roll their eyes. To them, the Holy Spirit is a biblical figure that doesn't have much to do with their faith today. Others scratch their heads. They don't know much about the Holy Spirit or understand who he is and what he does in their lives.

No matter where you fall on this spectrum, this session will help you understand who the Holy Spirit *actually* is and how he can *actually* help in your life. (Because we could all use a little help from our friends, right?) You will discover that when it comes to your need for *supernatural* help, the Holy Spirit is your best friend.

He didn't just exist in the book of Acts. He isn't a mysterious figure that you can never get to know. The Holy Spirit is here, alive, and well, moving and breathing in you and through you—and his power will help you.

10 min

Share

If you or any of your group members don't know each other, take a few minutes to introduce yourselves. Then, to get things started, discuss one of the following questions:

- What do you do when you need help with the bigger challenges in life?

— *or* —

- What thoughts or images come up when you hear the name *Holy Spirit*?

10 min

Read

At the start of each session, you will be given a passage of Scripture to read that relates to the key themes and ideas that will be presented in the video teaching. Break into groups of two to three people to read through this passage, and then take a few minutes to write down your responses to the questions that follow. Share your answers before you rejoin the main group.

> *If you love me, keep my commands. And I will ask the Father, and he will give you another advocate to help you and be with you forever—the Spirit of truth. The world cannot accept him, because it neither sees him nor knows him. But you know him, for he lives with you and will be in you.*
>
> John 14:15–17

- What does Jesus instruct his followers to do if they love him? Why do you think that he emphasizes this point to his disciples?

- Jesus told his disciples they already knew the Holy Spirit. Do you feel like you *know* the Holy Spirit? Why or why not?

Watch

Now it's time to watch the video for this session, which you can access by playing the DVD or through streaming (see the instructions printed on the inside front cover). Fill in the blanks below as you follow along, and also record any thoughts that stand out to you. (See the answer key at the end of this group section if you get stuck or miss any of these blanks.)

1. Followers of Christ have been given access to the _____ _____. Just like a big brother, he chooses each day to be our powerful _____.

2. The Holy Spirit is the executor of God's will, come to infuse us with _____. He equips us not to just get by but to actually _____, shine forth, and live the abundant life that Jesus spoke about so often.

3. Challenges come with life, but they need not _____ your life. Help is here. And he comes with the promise of _____.

4. The power of the Holy Spirit does not only apply to us as _____. Yes, the Spirit is always there to fill us when we approach him. But sometimes he pours out his power over entire _____.

5. You can be a part of this great outflowing of power. A contributor to this raging _____. For you have something to offer to others who are _____.

6. When the Living Water of our Lord and Savior pours into our
_____, the Holy Spirit flows out of us and electrifies the
dead places of the world. This is how _____ happens.

Discuss

Take some time to discuss what you just watched by answering the following questions.

1. Do you have an ally in your life—someone who is on your side and supports you? If so, how does it feel to have that person in your life?

2. From what you know about the Holy Spirit, how could he be an ally for you?

3. Read aloud John 14:16. How is the Holy Spirit described in this passage? How have you experienced the Holy Spirit in this same way?

4. Read aloud Acts 1:4 and 8. How is the Holy Spirit described in this passage? How have you experienced the Holy Spirit in the way that he is described here?

5. Read Isaiah 44:3–5. How does this passage speak differently about the Holy Spirit as compared to the other two passages? Describe a time, if any, that you felt the Spirit's power flow out of you or you felt the Holy Spirit's power flow from someone else.

6. How do you hope this study will impact your understanding of the Holy Spirit?

Respond

The Bible records more than a dozen metaphors to describe the work of the Holy Spirit. On your own, look up the following passages listed under each of the images below. Then write down what the verse says about that particular role of the Holy Spirit.

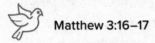 Matthew 3:16–17

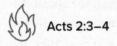 Acts 2:3–4

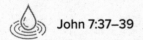 John 7:37–39

10 min

Pray

End your group time asking if anyone has any prayer requests to share. Write those requests down in the space below so you and your group members can pray about them in the week ahead. Finish by asking one person from the group to close your time in prayer.

Name	Request

WATCH ANSWERS: (1) Holy Spirit, ally; (2) strength, thrive; (3) define, power; (4) individuals, communities; (5) flood, thirsty; (6) hearts, revival

Personal Study

You are on a journey toward a better understanding of the Holy Spirit and his work in your life. A key part of that growth, regardless of where you are spiritually, involves studying Scripture. This is the goal of these personal studies—to help you explore what the Bible has to say and how to apply God's Word to your life. As you work through each of these personal studies, be sure to write down your responses to the questions (you will be given a few minutes to share your insight at the start of the next session if you are doing this study with others). Also, if you are reading through *Help Is Here* alongside this study, you may want to first review chapter 1.

1 The Holy Spirit for Dummies

The Holy Spirit can feel like an anomaly even if you have been a Christian for a long time. So today, spend some time taking inventory on what you know and believe about the Holy

Spirit and where those beliefs came from. Remember, you are not alone in your questions or misunderstandings of the Holy Spirit. Jesus' own disciples had questions about him! Read how Jesus explained the nature of the Spirit to his followers in the following passages.

> **John 14:16:** *"And I will ask the Father, and he will give you another advocate to help you and be with you forever."*

> **John 14:26:** *"But the Advocate, the Holy Spirit, whom the Father will send in my name, will teach you all things and will remind you of everything I have said to you."*

> **John 15:26:** *"When the Advocate comes, whom I will send to you from the Father—the Spirit of truth who goes out from the Father—he will testify about me."*

> **John 16:7:** *"But very truly I tell you, it is for your good that I am going away. Unless I go away, the Advocate will not come to you; but if I go, I will send him to you."*

1. When did you first learn about the Holy Spirit? What were you taught?

2. How is the Holy Spirit described in these passages? List any descriptor words or phrases.

3. The word *advocate* is a translation of the Greek work *parakletos*, which means encouragement. According to these verses, how does the Spirit encourage you?

4. What is something new you learned about the Holy Spirit from these verses?

Prayer: *Holy Spirit, guide me as I work through this study. Teach me about you and how you are working in my life. Speak to me in ways I can understand. Take away my fear or misunderstanding and replace it with curiosity. May my relationship with you deepen as I learn to depend on you. In Jesus' name I pray, amen.*

2 The Holy Spirit in the Old Testament

We often associate the Holy Spirit with Jesus' time on earth and after he ascended into heaven. This is understandable, since as you learned in yesterday's study, Jesus did talk about leaving us with the Holy Spirit after he left. But the Spirit existed long before Jesus came to earth. In fact, he is mentioned frequently in the Old Testament. Read the passages below and see what you can learn from these Old Testament writers and how they related to the Holy Spirit.

Ezekiel 36:26–27: *"I will give you a new heart and put a new spirit in you; I will remove from you your heart of stone and give you a heart of flesh. And I will put my Spirit in you and move you to follow my decrees and be careful to keep my laws."*

Psalm 139:7–10: *Where can I go from your Spirit? Where can I flee from your presence? If I go up to the heavens, you are there; if I make my bed in the depths, you are there. If I rise on the wings of the dawn, if I settle on the far side of the sea, even there your hand will guide me, your right hand will hold me fast.*

Nehemiah 9:19–20: *"Because of your great compassion you did not abandon them in the wilderness. By day the pillar of cloud did not fail to guide them on their path, nor the pillar of fire by night to shine on the way they were to take. You gave your good Spirit to instruct them. You did not withhold your manna from their mouths, and you gave them water for their thirst."*

1. Before reading these passages, what role did you think the Holy Spirit played before the coming of Christ?

2. How is the Holy Spirit described in these passages?

3. According to Ezekiel 36:26–27 and Nehemiah 9:19–20, how does the Spirit guide us?

4. Does knowing the Holy Spirit is present throughout Scripture, and not just in the New Testament, change the way you think about or understand him? If so, how?

Prayer: *"Where can I go from your Spirit? Where can I flee from your presence? If I go up to the heavens, you are there; if I make my bed in the depths, you are there. If I rise on the wings of the dawn, if I settle on the far side of the sea, even there your hand will guide me, your right hand will hold me fast" (Psalm 139:7–10). In Jesus' name, amen.*

3 The Holy Spirit As Your Ally

Burnout, stress, and anxiety can take over our lives if we're not careful. Whether it's stress about work, family, politics, or finances, it's easy to fall into the trap of thinking that we have to keep it all together all the time—that everything is up to *us*. But this just leads to more stress. Perhaps you know what it's like to hit a wall or be at the end of your rope. But when you're in a difficult season, you can always find hope in the Holy Spirit. He is your ally—someone who is there for you to support you. He can help take the load off so you can rest and feel peace. Read what Paul says in Romans about how the Spirit can be your ally in times of need:

> **Romans 8:5–11:** *Those who live according to the flesh have their minds set on what the flesh desires; but those who live in accordance with the Spirit have their minds set on what the Spirit desires. The mind governed by the flesh is death, but the mind governed by the Spirit is life and peace. The mind governed by the flesh is hostile to God; it does not submit to God's law, nor can it do so. Those who are in the realm of the flesh cannot please God.*
>
> *You, however, are not in the realm of the flesh but are in the realm of the Spirit, if indeed the Spirit of God lives in you. And if anyone does not have the Spirit of Christ, they do not belong to Christ. But if Christ is in you, then even though your body is subject to death because of sin, the Spirit gives life because of righteousness. And if the Spirit of him who raised Jesus from the dead is living in you, he who raised Christ from the dead will also give life to your mortal bodies because of his Spirit who lives in you.*

1. Describe a time in your life when you felt burned out or overwhelmed. How did you try to cope with that burn out?

2. According to this passage, what is the difference between living in the flesh and living in the Spirit?

3. Think about a personal experience you have with living according to your flesh. How could the Spirit have helped you during that time?

4. What is something new you learned about the flesh and the Spirit from this passage?

Prayer: *Holy Spirit, thank you for being my ally. May I rely on you during my times of need. I often feel anxious and overwhelmed by what's going on in my life. I feel like it is up to me to fix it. Help me not rely on my flesh but rather on you to get me through. Bring me peace during times of anxiety and hope during times of distress. Remind me to rely on your power and not my own. In Jesus' name, amen.*

4 Thriving in the Spirit

Have you ever driven home, pulled into your driveway, and realized you don't remember how you got there? You were on autopilot, and muscle memory kicked in to get you home. You can live your life this way as well—on autopilot, unaware of what's really going on around you, and unaware of the depth of life that Jesus is inviting you to experience. The Holy Spirit can help you live a life where you're not just surviving on autopilot, but you're actually *thriving*. Read what the Bible says about this invitation you have to thrive in Christ.

> **John 10:10:** *"The thief comes only to steal and kill and destroy; I have come that they may have life, and have it to the full."*

> **Romans 15:13:** *May the God of hope fill you with all joy and peace as you trust in him, so that you may overflow with hope by the power of the Holy Spirit.*

> **Ephesians 1:19–20:** *I also pray that you will understand the incredible greatness of God's power for us who believe him. This is the same mighty power that raised Christ from*

the dead and seated him in the place of honor at God's right hand in the heavenly realms (NLT).

2 Corinthians 5:17: *Therefore, if anyone is in Christ, the new creation has come: The old has gone, the new is here!*

1. Are you on autopilot right now, or do you feel like you're thriving? Explain.

2. According to these verses that you just read, what can the Christian life look like?

3. From what you've learned about the Holy Spirit so far, how can he make this sort of life possible?

4. In what areas of your life do you need the Holy Spirit to help you go from surviving to thriving?

Prayer: *God, you have made abundant life possible through the power of your Spirit. The same Spirit that conquered the grave lives in me—what a promise! Help me to believe in that promise today. Life can feel so monotonous. I can feel indifferent to my work, my family, and my community. But I don't want to live on autopilot. Allow your Spirit to work in me and show me what I can so easily miss in my life. May I appreciate what you have given me and feel a sense of passion for all that I have. In Jesus' name, and by the power of the Holy Spirit, I pray, amen.*

For Next Session: *Write down any insights or questions you want to discuss at the next group meeting. In preparation for the next session, read chapters 3 and 7 in* Help Is Here.

Our Strength and Guide

"I will give you a new heart—I will give you new and right desires—and put a new spirit within you. I will take out your stony hearts of sin and give you new hearts of love. And I will put my Spirit within you so that you will obey my laws and do whatever I command."

EZEKIEL 36:26–27 TLB

Welcome

Our cultural cliches reveal a lot about how we feel about work and accomplishments. We can *do it all*. *Pull ourselves up by our bootstraps. Pursue our dreams. The sky's the limit.*

In the right context, these can be encouraging phrases that lift us up. They can make us feel capable of doing more than we think we are capable of achieving in the moment. They can motivate us. But these cliches can also leave us feeling exhausted, can't they?

I should be able to *do it all* . . . so why does everything feel so hard right now?

All I need to do is *pull myself up by my bootstraps* . . . so what am I not even sure that I even have the strength for one more day?

If *the sky's the limit* . . . why does my energy, time, and passion feel so limited?

The reality is that as humans, there's only so much we can do before we run into other cliches like *hitting a wall, running out of steam*, or not knowing how we will *make ends meet*. It's tempting to blame ourselves during such times. We're not strong enough, rich enough, or good enough. But hitting a wall doesn't mean we're doing something wrong—it simply means we're relying on the wrong person. We're relying on ourselves rather than the Holy Spirit.

The Holy Spirit is here to help you, and when you run out of steam, he can give you what you need. Not sure you can forgive that family member? Ask the Holy Spirit to help you. Feel low on love and high on frustration with your toddler? Ask the Holy Spirit to fill you with love. At a difficult crossroads in life and not sure what to do next? Ask the Holy Spirit to guide you.

In today's session, you will look at two different types of faith: *rowboat* faith and *powerboat* faith. Rowboat faith requires you to strain at the oars and do all the work. But powerboat faith has a motor who does the work for you. This motor is the Holy Spirit.

Now, powerboat faith doesn't guarantee a worry-free, stress-free, or struggle-free existence. But it does promise you the presence of the Spirit within these worries. And it contains the promise of delivery by the Holy Spirit's strength, rather than your own.

Both boats await you at the dock. Which one will you choose?

Share

Welcome to session two of the *Help Is Here* study. If you or any of your group members are not yet acquainted, take a few minutes to introduce yourselves and share any insights you have from your personal study. Then, to kick things off, discuss one of the following questions:

* What kind of faith do you have today—rowboat faith or powerboat faith?

— *or* —

* Describe a time in your life when you had either rowboat faith or powerboat faith. Why did you turn to this type of faith at that time?

Read

Break into groups of two to three people to read through the following passage from the Gospel of John, and then take a few minutes to write down your responses to the questions that follow. Share your answers with each other before you rejoin the main group.

> *"Very truly I tell you, no one can enter the kingdom of God unless they are born of water and the Spirit. Flesh gives birth to flesh, but the Spirit gives birth to spirit. You should not be surprised at my saying, 'You must be born again.' The wind blows wherever it pleases. You hear its sound, but you cannot tell where it comes from or where it is going. So it is with everyone born of the Spirit."*
>
> John 3:5–8

- This passage relates a conversation that Jesus had with a Jewish religious leader named Nicodemus. What requirement does Jesus give to Nicodemus as it relates to entering into the kingdom of God?

- Why do you think Jesus told Nicodemus that he "should not be surprised" when he said that Nicodemus must be "born again"?

Watch

Now watch the video for this session (remember that you can access this video via streaming by following the instructions printed on the inside front cover). Once again, fill in the blanks below as you follow along with the teaching, and record any thoughts that stand out to you.

1. We dare not think for a minute that we have the _____ in and of ourselves to be the people God calls us to be. But we must also not think for a minute that he will not _____ us for the task.

2. Nicodemus was obsessed with what a person *can* and *cannot* do. He was all about _____ effort, _____ gumption, _____ achievement. In his view, the gate to heaven was opened with elbow grease.

3. Where _____ Christianity fails, _____ Christianity thrives. Instead of relying on our own efforts, we rely on God. The Holy Spirit is the spark in our engine that drives us forward and equips us to do all the things that God wants us to do.

4. The difference between rowing your own boat and _____ in the Spirit is not ease, but _____.

5. The _____ is the primary communication tool of the Holy Spirit. God will speak to you through its pages. His will is found in his _____.

6. God didn't put you here on this earth to go it alone. You're part of a community called the _____. Your captain is none other than your heavenly Father. So learn to hear his _____.

Discuss

Take some time to discuss what you just watched by answering the following questions.

1. Read John 3:1–12. What is Nicodemus' status in the Jewish community? Why is this important to know in the context of his conversation with Jesus?

2. What does it mean to be born of the Spirit, as Jesus talked about in this passage?

3. Do you feel you have been born again of the Spirit? Why or why not?

4. What are two strategies for discerning the will of the Holy Spirit?

5. Which of these strategies do you most naturally use? Explain.

6. How has your faith community helped you in doing the work God has called you to do?

Respond

Think about the two types of faith presented in this session: *rowboat* faith and *powerboat* faith. Below the image of the rowboat, write down three ways that you tend to act out of your *own power* when facing difficult situations. Then, below the image of the powerboat, write down three ways that you will seek to rely on the Holy Sprit's power when facing these situations.

1.

2.

3.

1.

2.

3.

Pray

End your time by leading your group in prayer, or pray the following prayer aloud together:

Holy Spirit, we often try to make it in this life alone, trying to muscle our way through the hard times and difficulties, rowing our own boats until we are too tired to do it anymore. Teach us how to rely on your Spirit for strength and guidance. Relieve our anxiety as we give our concerns to you. Remind us that every fear, regret, and worry has already been laid at the feet of Jesus on the cross. In his name we pray, amen.

Ask if anyone has any prayer requests to share. Write those requests down in the space below so you and your group members can pray about them in the week ahead.

Name   Request

_____ _____

_____ _____

_____ _____

_____ _____

_____ _____

_____ _____

_____ _____

WATCH ANSWERS: (1) POWER, EQUIP; (2) HUMAN, HUMAN, HUMAN; (3) ROWBOAT, POWERBOAT; (4) TRUSTING, EFFECTIVENESS; (5) BIBLE, WORD; (6) CHURCH, VOICE

Personal Study

A s you discussed in your group time this week, "rowboat" Christianity only exhausts and frustrates. Those who attempt it—straining at the oars of their own efforts—find themselves depleted and desperate at the attempt. But those who look to the *Holy Spirit* to do the work find fresh power. Life still has storms. The water grows rough. The wind still howls at times. But when we rely on the Holy Spirit, we are never left to face the fury on our own.

1 Walking by the Spirit

Rowboat faith is deceiving. At first, it can appear to be working. You're exerting great effort. You have energy and stamina. You are helpful when others need you. You love those who are difficult to love. Perhaps you even forgive your friends and family when they wrong you because you know that's what you are supposed to do. Yes, rowboat faith works . . . until it doesn't. Inevitably, even the most faithful follower will get tired of rowing and trying and white-knuckling the virtues of the Christian life. The reality is that we were never meant to force love, or force forgiveness, or force humility from within ourselves. We were meant to rely on the one who was sent to help and *walk with him*. Read what Paul says about this in Galatians:

> **Galatians 5:16–25:** *So I say, walk by the Spirit, and you will not gratify the desires of the flesh. For the flesh desires what is contrary to the Spirit, and the Spirit what is contrary to the flesh. They are in conflict with each other, so that you are not to do whatever you want. But if you are led by the Spirit, you are not under the law.*
>
> *The acts of the flesh are obvious: sexual immorality, impurity and debauchery; idolatry and witchcraft; hatred, discord, jealousy, fits of rage, selfish ambition, dissensions, factions and envy; drunkenness, orgies, and the like. I warn you, as I did before, that those who live like this will not inherit the kingdom of God.*
>
> *But the fruit of the Spirit is love, joy, peace, forbearance, kindness, goodness, faithfulness, gentleness and self-control. Against such things there is no law. Those who belong to Christ Jesus have crucified the flesh with its passions and desires. Since we live by the Spirit, let us keep in step with the Spirit.*

1. When you are running low on love, forgiveness, mercy, grace, or other Christian virtues, what do you typically do?

2. According to this passage, how do you develop the fruits of the Spirit?

3. Underline the fruit of the Spirit that Paul lists in verses 22–23. Which of these characteristics do you wish was more developed in you? Why?

4. What does it mean to "walk by the Spirit." How could you walk by the Spirit today?

Prayer: *Lord, I confess to you any sins of the flesh in my life—immorality, impurity, hatred, discord, jealousy, selfishness, and the like. I pray that you will help me to walk by the power of the Spirit so I can witness the fruit of the Spirit in my life—love, joy, peace, forbearance, kindness, goodness, faithfulness, gentleness, and self-control. In Jesus' name, amen.*

2 At a Crossroads

The Holy Spirit doesn't only give you strength to live the Christian life, but he also acts as a guide when you are trying to make a decision or when you find yourself in an uncertain time and don't know what to do next. Making decisions is stressful—especially if it is a decision that could significantly change your life, like a move, or a new job, or a life partner. But you don't have make decisions alone, and you don't have to fear that you're making the wrong decisions. The Holy Spirit will lead you. Read about Paul's experience with this in the book of Acts:

> **Acts 16:6–15:** *Paul and his companions traveled throughout the region of Phrygia and Galatia, having been kept by the Holy Spirit from preaching the word in the province of Asia. When they came to the border of Mysia, they tried to enter Bithynia, but the Spirit of Jesus would not allow them to. So they passed by Mysia and went down to Troas. During the night Paul had a vision of a man of Macedonia standing and begging him, "Come over to Macedonia and help us." After Paul had seen the vision, we got ready at once to leave for Macedonia, concluding that God had called us to preach the gospel to them.*
>
> *From Troas we put out to sea and sailed straight for Samothrace, and the next day we went on to Neapolis. From there we traveled to Philippi, a Roman colony and the leading city of that district of Macedonia. And we stayed there several days.*
>
> *On the Sabbath we went outside the city gate to the river, where we expected to find a place of prayer. We sat down and began to speak to the women who had gathered there. One of those listening was a woman from the city of Thyatira named Lydia, a dealer in purple cloth. She was a worshiper of God. The Lord opened her heart to respond to*

Paul's message. When she and the members of her household were baptized, she invited us to her home.

1. Have you ever felt the Spirit leading you to do something, go somewhere, or speak to someone? If so, how did you respond to that leading?

2. Where did the Holy Spirit lead, and not lead, Paul and his companions in this passage? How do you think Paul discerned the will of the Spirit as he travelled?

3. What was the result of Paul's following the Holy Spirit's leading?

4. What does this passage tell you about how the Holy Spirit can lead you and what happens as a result if you follow the Spirit?

Prayer: *Lord, you are my shepherd. I lack nothing. You make me lie down in green pastures. You lead me beside quiet waters. You refresh my soul. You guide me along the right paths. Even though I walk through the darkest valley, I can fear no evil, for you are with me. Your rod and your staff, they comfort me. You prepare a table before me in the presence of my enemies. You anoint my head with oil; my cup overflows. Surely your goodness and love will follow me all the days of my life, and I will dwell in your house forever (see Psalm 23:1–6). In Jesus' name, amen.*

3 Go to the Verse

It is one thing to *say* that you will start relying on the Holy Spirit. It is another to actually put this into practice. After all, practically speaking, how can you know where the Spirit is leading you? How can you know if it is the *Spirit* leading you, or if your own *desires* are leading you, or if you are hearing the voices of others? One way to discern the voice of the Spirit is to "go to the verse." Seek your answer in Scripture. God's Word is your true north and is truth that you can trust. So, if you're not sure what to do next or you feel unsure about a decision you've made, turn to Scripture. Read the following verses about God's Word and the role it can play in your life:

> **Psalm 1:1–3:** *How well God must like you—you don't walk in the ruts of those blind-as-bats, you don't stand with the good-for-nothings, you don't take your seat among the know-it-alls. Instead you thrill to GOD's Word, you chew on Scripture day and night. You're a tree replanted in Eden,*

bearing fresh fruit every month, Never dropping a leaf, always in blossom (MSG).

Psalm 119:105: *Your word is a lamp for my feet, a light on my path.*

Romans 15:4: *For everything that was written in the past was written to teach us, so that through the endurance taught in the Scriptures and the encouragement they provide we might have hope.*

Hebrews 4:12: *For the word of God is alive and active. Sharper than any double-edged sword, it penetrates even to dividing soul and spirit, joints and marrow; it judges the thoughts and attitudes of the heart.*

1. What is your relationship like with Scripture? Are you close to it, reading it every day? Or are you far from it, letting your Bible collect dust on a shelf? Or are you somewhere in between these extremes?? Explain your answer.

2. What metaphors do these passages use to describe God's Word? How do they help you understand the uses for and the purpose of Scripture?

3. According to Romans 15:4, what should the word ultimately give you?

4. Do you feel hope when you read God's Word? Why or
why not?

Prayer: *Holy Spirit, I confess I often turn to my own wisdom and
discernment when trying to make a decision. Teach me to turn to
God's Word. Speak to me through this book that can be difficult to
understand. Reveal your will through it, reveal teaching that will help
me, and refine me. Give me insights as I read so I can have a deeper
understanding of who you are and what you want for my life. Thank
you for speaking to me in this way. Give me ears to hear. Amen.*

4 Go to the Voice

The Holy Spirit will guide you when you "go to the verse" and
"go to the voice"—the voice of God. God still speaks today.
Now, it might not seem this is the case, because his voice isn't
booming down from heaven, or he isn't speaking from a
burning bush, but his voice can still be heard by his followers.
And his voice can reach you in a few different ways. So, let's
go to the verse to better understand how to *go to the voice* by
reading the following verses:

Isaiah 30:21: *Whether you turn to the right or to the left, your ears will hear a voice behind you, saying, "This is the way; walk in it."*

John 8:47: *"Whoever belongs to God hears what God says. The reason you do not hear is that you do not belong to God."*

John 10:27–28: *"My sheep listen to my voice; I know them, and they follow me. I give them eternal life, and they shall never perish; no one will snatch them out of my hand."*

1. Have you ever heard the voice of God? If so, how did you know it was God?

2. According to Isaiah 30:21, what can the voice of God tell you?

3. According to John 8:47 and John 10:27–28, who can hear God's voice? Why do you think this is the case?

4. What do you need to hear from God? What question or concern do you have that he could speak into today?

Prayer: *Sit in stillness for several minutes as your prayer time today. Listen for the voice of God. Spend more time listening than talking. Wait and see what the Holy Spirit reveals.*

For Next Session: *Write down any insights or questions you want to discuss at the next group meeting. In preparation for the next session, read chapters 5 and 6 in* Help Is Here.

Our Peace and Guarantee

*"I am leaving you with a gift—peace of mind and heart!
And the peace I give isn't fragile like the peace the world
gives. So don't be troubled or afraid."*

JOHN 14:27 TLB

Welcome

W e aren't guaranteed much in this life. Perhaps you know what it's like to think you have your life planned out—the school, the job, the partner, the kids, the perfect health, the robust savings account—and for some or all of these not to go the way you that thought. It seems the older we get, the less guarantees we have. But there is one guarantee on which we all can depend . . . and it is the greatest guarantee of our lives, both on this earth and in the life to come.

In this session, we will look at what it means to be "sealed" by the Holy Spirit. While this might not be a familiar term to us today, it is how Paul described one of the key functions of the Holy Spirit. As he wrote, "When you believed, you were marked in him with a seal, the promised Holy Spirit, who is a deposit guaranteeing our inheritance" (Ephesians 1:13–14). This guarantee is like a down payment, assuring us of what we have through Christ and who we are through Christ—saved from our sins, beloved children of God, inheritors of his kingdom.

How would your life change if you really *believed* in this inheritance? Maybe life has left you convinced that you don't deserve anything or that you will never get what you deserve. But with the mark of the Holy Spirit, you are guaranteed a God-sized inheritance. You are a part of his family. You are assured of all that you could ever need now and in the future.

When you believe in this guarantee and this new identity you have in the Spirit, you can let go of the fear and anxiety that all of those other lost guarantees have caused you. You can renew your faith in a God who loves you, cares for you, and is providing all that you need. You no longer have to walk in disappointment and angst, convinced that life has no guarantees. For while this world may not provide such assurances, your heavenly Father certainly does.

Share

Welcome to session three of the *Help Is Here* study. To get things started for this week's group time, discuss one of the following questions:

- What did you once think was a guarantee in life—but now no longer do?

  — *or* —

- What are some fears or anxieties right now that you would like to be rid of?

Read

Break into groups of two to three people to read through the following passage from the Gospel of Matthew, and then take a few minutes to write down your responses to the questions that follow. Share your answers with each other before you rejoin the main group.

Then Jesus came from Galilee to the Jordan to be baptized by John. But John tried to deter him, saying, "I need to be baptized by you, and do you come to me?"

Jesus replied, "Let it be so now; it is proper for us to do this to fulfill all righteousness." Then John consented.

As soon as Jesus was baptized, he went up out of the water. At that moment heaven was opened, and he saw the Spirit of God descending like a dove and alighting on him. And a voice from heaven said, "This is my Son, whom I love; with him I am well pleased."

Matthew 3:13–17

- What was John's reaction when he saw Jesus standing on the shore of the Jordan River?

- What does this passage reveal about Jesus' relationship with the Holy Spirit?

Watch

Now watch the video for this session. Fill in the blanks below as you follow along with the teaching and record any thoughts or ideas that stand out to you.

1. The Holy Spirit is the _____ presence of God in the world today. He will help us defy the voices of _____ and come into his presence of peace.

2. The inaugural activity of the Holy Spirit was to hover over a _____ world. When we turn to the New Testament, we find this same _____.

3. There are times in which our spirits are troubled and _____. We long for the tranquil assurance of a loving _____. For this, we turn to the Holy Spirit.

4. Sealing is the act that says: "This is mine, and this is protected." The Holy Spirit's work is in sealing not only your present _____, but also your future _____.

5. Your salvation, and your eternal inheritance, are _____
   by God's Spirit. You will never lose them. You will never be
   separated from God. You can take that _____ to the bank.

6. Even in a world defined by _____, we are undeniably
   God's own children. We can persevere through the _____
   that rage not only around us, but also inside us.

Discuss

Take some time to discuss what you just watched by answering the following questions.

1. Talk about a chaotic season that you have had in your
   life. What happened and how did you get through it?

2. According to Genesis 1:2, what role did the Holy Spirit play in creation? How could the Holy Spirit play this role in your own seasons of chaos?

3. Read Romans 8:14–15. Considering the historical context of this verse, what is the significance of adoption?

4. How does knowing that you belong to a family, community, or group of friends affect your identity and how you feel about yourself?

5. How could knowing you belong to God in this same way affect the way that you feel about yourself?

6. What promise of the Holy Spirit do you need most right now—the Spirit who comforts as a mother, or the Spirit who guarantees your identity as adopted sons of God?

Respond

Take a few minutes on your own to further reflect on the idea of the Holy Spirit as a "guarantee" or "seal" of your salvation. Look up each passage listed below and briefly write down what it says about this particular role of the Holy Spirit.

 2 Corinthians 1:21–22

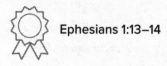 **Ephesians 1:13–14**

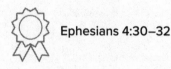 **Ephesians 4:30–32**

Pray

End your time by leading your group in prayer, or pray the following prayer aloud together:

> *Dear God, we know that you are our good Father. You have adopted us as your own, guaranteeing our inheritance through the work of your Spirit. Because of this, we have nothing to fear. We have nothing to be anxious about. When the fear and anxiety do come, comfort us as a mother comforts her child. Be near to us and hold us until the chaos subsides.*

We know that the guarantee is not that our lives will be worry free but that you will be with us in the midst of the worry. For this, we are grateful. In Jesus' name we pray, amen.

Ask if anyone has any prayer requests to share. Write those requests down in the space below so you and your group members can pray about them in the week ahead.

Name   Request

_____   _____

_____   _____

_____   _____

_____   _____

_____   _____

_____   _____

_____   _____

_____   _____

WATCH ANSWERS: (1) CALMING, FEAR; (2) FRENZIED, IMAGE; (3) ANXIOUS, MOTHER; (4) SALVATION, BLESSING; (5) GUARANTEED, TRUTH; (6) CHAOS, STORMS

Personal Study

As you discussed in your group time this week, God has sealed you with the Spirit. *Sealed.* You know the verb. You twist a jar lid to *seal* the pickles. You lick an envelope to *seal* the letter. You notarize the contract to *seal* the deal. Sealing declares ownership and secures contents. Sealing is the act through which God says of you, "This is mine . . . and this is protected."

1 Calm in the Chaos

Anxiety affects all of us. It is a part of the human life. We worry about big and small things. Sometimes we have anxious days. Sometimes we have anxious seasons. Sometimes anxiety seems to plague us for years. But no matter what type of anxiety you may be experiencing right now, you have the antidote to anxiety: the Holy Spirit. The Spirit can comfort you and reassure you during the most anxious times of your life, as this psalm from David relates:

Psalm 131:1–3: *My heart is not proud, LORD, my eyes are not haughty; I do not concern myself with great matters or things too wonderful for me. But I have calmed and quieted myself, I am like a weaned child with its mother; like a weaned child I am content. Israel, put your hope in the LORD both now and forevermore.*

1. David wrote, "I do not concern myself with great matters or things too wonderful for me" (verse 1). What is a "great matter" causing you anxiety right now? How have you been coping with this anxiety?

2. What is the significance of David comparing himself to a weaned child with its mother?

3. How do you feel about the Spirit or God being associated with a mother? Why?

4. What sort of motherly comfort do you need right now? Why?

Prayer: *Heavenly Father, I declare today that my heart is not proud, nor my eyes haughty. I do not concern myself with great matters or things too wonderful for me. But I have calmed and quieted myself, I am like a weaned child with its mother; like a weaned child I am content. I will put my hope in you, both now and forevermore (see Psalm 131:1–3).*

2 There Is One Guarantee

The Holy Spirit calms your anxiety by being your guarantee. In the Spirit, you have the greatest guarantee of all: the inheritance of God's kingdom. As you experience disappointment in life, it's easy to believe that *nothing* is guaranteed. However, because of Christ, and through the power of the Holy Spirit, you can rest assured you have everything you need. Paul explained how the Holy Spirit serves as the guarantee of your salvation in his letter to the Ephesians:

> **Ephesians 1:11–14:** *In him we were also chosen, having been predestined according to the plan of him who works out everything in conformity with the purpose of his will, in order that we, who were the first to put our hope in Christ, might be for the praise of his glory. And you also were*

included in Christ when you heard the message of truth, the gospel of your salvation. When you believed, you were marked in him with a seal, the promised Holy Spirit, who is a deposit guaranteeing our inheritance until the redemption of those who are God's possession—to the praise of his glory.

1. What is something you thought was guaranteed in your life that has turned out not to be guaranteed? (You may have answered this in your group time but go into further detail here). How has this affected your faith in God and in others?

2. What role does the Holy Spirit play in this passage?

3. In the original Greek, the word *guarantee* meant a down payment. The Holy Spirit acts as a down payment of the inheritance you will ultimately receive in heaven. How does this affect the way you view salvation? How does this affect the way you view God?

4. What guarantee do you need most from God today? Do you believe the Holy Spirit can assure this guarantee? Why or why not?

Prayer: *Dear Father, I confess that at times I have lost faith in my friends, my family, and even in you. Life can feel so hard. I've experienced so much disappointment. It seems nothing is a guarantee, and I have lost hope. But I know the Holy Spirit has guaranteed the one promise I really need: living with you forever in eternity. May this future promise give me present hope. May I remember it when I lose faith. May this guarantee help me believe more in you, in others, and in myself. Thank you for this great promise I have in you. In your Son's name I pray, amen.*

3 A Good Father
• • •

The Holy Spirit not only guarantees your inheritance but also guarantees your identity as a child of God. Paul wrote, "The Spirit you received brought about your adoption to sonship" (Romans 8:15). Under Roman law, adoption significantly changed children's identity. They lost all connection to their old family and gained all the rights to their new family. They became heirs to their father's estate. They were forgiven any prior debts and were treated as legitimate children of their new father. Being in Christ and marked by the Holy Spirit changes your identity in the same way that adoption changed a child's identity. Read the rest of this passage:

Romans 8:14–17: *For those who are led by the Spirit of God are the children of God. The Spirit you received does not make you slaves, so that you live in fear again; rather, the Spirit you received brought about your adoption to sonship. And by him we cry, "Abba, Father." The Spirit himself testifies with our spirit that we are God's children. Now if we are children, then we are heirs—heirs of God and co-heirs with Christ, if indeed we share in his sufferings in order that we may also share in his glory.*

1. How do you typically view your relationship with God? Why do you see God in this way?

2. According to verse 15, how should the truth of your adoption take away any tendency to live in fear?

3. According to verse 17, what does being God's child promise you?

4. The Holy Spirit makes it possible for God to be your father. List the attributes of a good father. Which of these attributes do you believe God has? Which ones do you *need* to believe God has?

Prayer: *Father, you are a good father. I believe I have been adopted by the power of the Holy Spirit. Even on the days I don't believe this is true, it still is because the Spirit testifies for me. Thank you so much for this promise. May I grow deeper in this belief. May I see you more and more as a good father. May my tainted views of a father not interfere with the way I see you, talk to you, and live by your Word. Thank you for being my father. In Jesus' name I pray, amen.*

4 Who Are You?

• • •

This week, you've read what the Bible says about how the Holy Spirit calms your anxiety, guarantees your salvation, and marks you as an adopted child of God. When you don't believe in this power of the Spirit, it can be easy to misplace your identity and overidentify with your anxieties, disappointments, and loneliness. But when you do this, you *become* your anxiety, your disappointments, or your loneliness, making it even harder to overcome these trials. The Bible assures you of the new identity made possible through the Spirit, and it assures you that this identity has stuck. You can't lose it. Read what Paul writes about this in Romans:

Romans 8:35–39: *Who shall separate us from the love of Christ? Shall trouble or hardship or persecution or famine or nakedness or danger or sword? As it is written: "For your sake we face death all day long; we are considered as sheep to be slaughtered." No, in all these things we are more than conquerors through him who loved us. For I am convinced that neither death nor life, neither angels nor demons, neither the present nor the future, nor any powers, neither height nor depth, nor anything else in all creation, will be able to separate us from the love of God that is in Christ Jesus our Lord.*

1. What do you tend to overidentify with the most—your anxiety, disappointment, loneliness, or something else? Explain.

2. Paul lists several obstacles in verses 37–39 that could convince you that you have lost the love of Christ and your identity as a child of God. Which of these have you feared could separate you from God's love? Why?

3. How does the promise in these verses calm your anxieties about your salvation?

4. What do you need to believe about your identity today? Why is this hard to believe about yourself?

Prayer: *Lord, I choose to believe that nothing can separate me from your love. I believe that in you, and through the power of the Holy Spirit, I am more than a conqueror. Help me to never lose sight of the fact that nothing—neither death nor life, neither angels nor demons, neither the present nor the future, nor any powers, neither height nor depth, nor anything else in all creation—can separate me from your love (see Romans 8:35–39). In Jesus' name, amen.*

For Next Session: *Write down any insights or questions you want to discuss at the next group meeting. In preparation for the next session, read chapters 4 and 9 in* Help Is Here.

Our Intercessor and Advocate

"Yet even now the witness to my innocence is there in heaven; my advocate is there on high."

JOB 16:19 TLB

Welcome

There are many things in this life that can leave us at a loss for words. Sometimes, it is the beauty of the moment that steals our breath away. Other times, it is the tragedy and pain of a moment that leaves us grasping for words of comfort or meaning.

You've surely experienced being at a loss for words in these moments. But have you ever experienced being at a loss for words in prayer? Maybe you hit your knees to pray for a friend, for yourself, or for a national tragedy—but nothing comes out. The moment is too big. The thing you are praying for is too hard. You don't know what to say to your heavenly Father because your needs are so many . . . or because you don't even *know* what you need.

What do you do in these moments? Do you give up, get up, and walk away? It's tempting to do so and just think that God is not with you in that moment and that, in the darkest times, he is the hardest to find. But the Bible tells us something different. In fact, the Scripture tells us that during such times, the Holy Spirit actually *intercedes* on your behalf. As the apostle Paul put it in Romans 8:26: "We do not know what we ought to pray for, but the Spirit himself intercedes for us through wordless groans."

What a relief! When you are at a loss for the words, the Holy Spirit within you is not. On the contrary, this is when he gets to work, praying on your behalf, saying the words to God that you cannot find. Sound crazy? Well, that's understandable, but the work of the Holy Spirit is mysterious and beyond us. We can't limit how or when the Spirit moves. When you've been anointed by the Spirit, as all are who have put their faith in Christ, amazing things can happen.

This anointing and intercessory work by the Holy Spirit are just two more ways that God shows you that he is with you, *always*, even in the dark moments when you are on your knees with no words to pray. When the pain is too much, the anguish too deep, God knows your pain. He knows your words will fall short, and in those moments his grace steps in, closing the gap between your need and your articulation of that need.

In this session, you will dig deeper into these workings of the Spirit: intercession and anointing. You will learn more about God's power and abilities. But most of all, you will be assured of his presence that never leaves you.

Share

Welcome to session four of the *Help Is Here* study. To get things started for this week's group time, discuss one of the following questions:

- When was the last time you were at a loss for words, either in prayer or when talking to someone else? How did it feel not to know what to say?

— or —

- What is your experience with anointing in the church? Is this something you grew up seeing in your community, or is it a new concept for you?

Read

Break into groups of two to three people to read through the following passage from the letter of Romans, and then take a few minutes to write down your responses to the questions that follow. Share your answers with each other before you rejoin the main group.

> We know that the whole creation has been groaning as in the pains of childbirth right up to the present time. Not only so, but we ourselves, who have the firstfruits of the Spirit, groan inwardly as we wait eagerly for our adoption to sonship, the redemption of our bodies. For in this hope we were saved. But hope that is seen is no hope at all. Who hopes for what they already have? But if we hope for what we do not yet have, we wait for it patiently.
>
> In the same way, the Spirit helps us in our weakness. We do not know what we ought to pray for, but the Spirit himself intercedes for us through wordless groans. And he who searches our hearts knows the mind of the Spirit, because the Spirit intercedes for God's people in accordance with the will of God.
>
> Romans 8:22–27

- What are some things you are "groaning inwardly" for right now?

- What are some of the ways the Spirit help you in your weakness?

Watch

Now watch the video for this session. Fill in the blanks below as you follow along with the teaching and record any thoughts or ideas that stand out to you.

1. The Bible tells us the raw appeals of our hearts find their way into the _____ of God. How can we be sure? Because they are _____ into the care of the Holy Spirit.

2. Each of us has a way that we would *like* to pray when we are in need. We want to pour out clear, _____, and passionate petitions before the throne of God. We desire to pray with power and _____, shaking the rooftops and forcing the enemy to flee.

3. The power the Holy Spirit provides enables us to do amazing things for God. Yet of equal importance is this _____ aspect of the Holy Spirit's nature. He curates our incoherent prayers borne of _____ into the tribunal of heaven.

4. Throughout the Bible, we find accounts of the Lord _____ his people that he loved them, was with them, and was working on their behalf. At times, the presence of God's Spirit was symbolized through an act known as _____ .

5. The moment you became a _____ of God, his grace covered you. His sovereignty stretched over you. The pathway to heaven was laid out before you. And the heart-healing oil of the Holy Spirit was _____ over your life.

6. When you pray, preach, prophesy, or live out your faith, you are _____ by the Holy Spirit's presence. So lean into him. You may grow _____ , but the Spirit never does.

Discuss

Take some time to discuss what you just watched by answering the following questions.

1. Has anyone ever interceded on your behalf like the friend did at the funeral in the opening story of the video? If so, how did that person's intercession affect you?

2. Re-read the apostle Paul's words in Romans 8:26–27. According to this passage, how and when does the Holy Spirit intercede for you?

3. Read Luke 4:14–19. What does Jesus say about the anointing that he received?

Anointed by the Spirit

4. How have followers of Christ likewise been anointed by God?

5. Have you felt God's anointing over your life? If so, in what way?

6. What is one way that you need the Holy Spirit to intercede for you today?

Respond

In the Bible, anointing with oil is often a symbol of the presence of God's Spirit. On your own, take a few minutes to read through the following stories of God anointing certain individuals in the Bible. Write down: (1) who was instructed to do the anointing, (2) who received the anointing, and (3) what that anointed person was supposed to do.

 Exodus 30:22, 30–33

Anointer:

Anointed:

Purpose of Anointing:

 1 Samuel 16:1, 10–13

Anointer:

Anointed:

Purpose of Anointing:

Acts 10:34–38

Anointer:

Anointed:

Purpose of Anointing:

Pray

End your meeting with an extended time of prayer as a group. Share requests and take turns allowing each person to pray aloud for them as he or she feels led. Act as each other's intercessors. Then leave a few moments of silence after praying for each request to allow the Holy Spirit to intercede on that person's behalf. If you have time, share with each other how this prayer time felt. Was it peaceful, uncomfortable . . . or something else? Did you feel the Holy Spirit's presence? How did it feel to have others intercede on your behalf? Finally, record any prayer requests from the group to pray about in the week ahead.

Name   Request

_____ _____
_____ _____
_____ _____
_____ _____
_____ _____
_____ _____
_____ _____
_____ _____
_____ _____

WATCH ANSWERS: (1) PRESENCE, ENTRUSTED; (2) ELOQUENT, CONFIDENCE; (3) GENTLE, GRIEF; (4) REASSURING, ANOINTING; (5) CHILD, POURED; (6) EMPOWERED, WEARY

Personal Study

As you discussed in your group time this week, we're accustomed to reading about the Holy Spirit's mighty deeds in the Bible. Fire falling on the disciples in the upper room. Jail doors opening for Paul. The Spirit caused dead bones to rise for Ezekiel and the Red Sea to open for Moses and the Israelites. Yet of equal import are the passages that revel the tender heart of the Holy Spirt. He curates and translates the prayers of the weak until they are heard in heaven.

1 The Groans of the Heart

Perhaps one of the most comforting characteristics of the Holy Spirit is his ability to speak on our behalf during our darkest moments when our heart can do nothing but groan. Sadness can be overwhelming. Despair can be daunting. Sometimes, our prayers are not made up of words at all. We simply throw up our hands in confusion or bow our heads in exhaustion. And this, according to Scripture, is okay. As

1 Samuel 16:7 says, "The LORD looks at the heart." God knows *your* heart when you have no words to tell him. He knows you are grieving, hurt, angry, or confused. And in those moments you can surrender, because an Advocate is speaking on your behalf. But remember who made this intervention possible. Jesus' death on the cross tore the veil between you and God, making the Almighty accessible to you at all times. Read the following verses that address how Jesus advocates for you in the throne room of God:

> **Hebrews 4:15–16:** *For we do not have a high priest who is unable to empathize with our weaknesses, but we have one who has been tempted in every way, just as we are—yet he did not sin. Let us then approach God's throne of grace with confidence, so that we may receive mercy and find grace to help us in our time of need.*

> **1 John 2:1–2:** *My dear children, I write this to you so that you will not sin. But if anybody does sin, we have an advocate with the Father—Jesus Christ, the Righteous One. He is the atoning sacrifice for our sins, and not only for ours but also for the sins of the whole world.*

1. What are some of your "groanings of the heart"—situations that are causing anxiety, sadness, anger, confusion, or despair? (You may have answered this during your group time but go into further detail here.)

2. According to Hebrews 4:16, what are you able to do and receive because of Jesus' intercession on your behalf?

3. According to 1 John 2:1–2, what was Jesus' ultimate act of advocacy on your behalf? How does this affect the way you view Jesus' ability to advocate for you in the struggles you are currently facing?

4. What areas of your life have you been relying on yourself to get through? How could you invite Jesus and the Holy Spirit to intercede on your behalf?

Prayer: *As you read above, sometimes prayers don't involve words but simply raising your hands in surrender or bowing your head in despair. When you don't have the words to pray, you can take a quiet walk, work on a painting, or simply sit under a tree and watch the branches as the wind blows through them. These acts can feed your soul when you don't have the words to say. Practice this type of prayer today. Do what feels most restful while being intentional.*

2 The Anointing of Kings
...

This week, you discussed the act of anointing as a way that God shows his people that he is with them and working on their behalf. While anointing may not be as common a practice in Christian churches today, in the Jewish tradition, it was a way of marking someone in a new role or identity. It was symbolic of God's power being with the person and a sign that he or she had been chosen by God to do it. Read a few other passages below that detail this ritual:

Exodus 29:4, 7–9: *Bring Aaron and his sons to the entrance to the tent of meeting and wash them with water.... Take the anointing oil and anoint him by pouring it on his head. Bring his sons and dress them in tunics and fasten caps on them. Then tie sashes on Aaron and his sons. The priesthood is theirs by a lasting ordinance.*

Psalm 45:1–2, 7: *My heart is stirred by a noble theme as I recite my verses for the king; my tongue is the pen of a skillful writer. You are the most excellent of men and your lips have been anointed with grace, since God has blessed you forever.... You love righteousness and hate wickedness; therefore God, your God, has set you above your companions by anointing you with the oil of joy.*

1 Chronicles 16:15–22: *He remembers his covenant forever, the promise he made, for a thousand generations, the covenant he made with Abraham, the oath he swore to Isaac. He confirmed it to Jacob as a decree, to Israel as an everlasting covenant: "To you I will give the land of Canaan as the* *portion you will inherit." When they were but few in number, few indeed, and strangers in it, they wandered from nation to nation, from one kingdom to another. He allowed no one to oppress them; for their sake he rebuked kings: "Do not touch my anointed ones; do my prophets no harm."*

1. Even if you've never been a part of an anointing ritual, what rituals or ceremonies does your community use to commemorate transitions like a new job title, a new role as a parent, retirement, and the like? Why do you think we practice these rituals ?

2. In the Exodus 29 passage, what did Aaron and his sons' anointing signify?

3. According to Psalm 45 and 1 Chronicles 16, what are some other ways God anointed his people? What did that mean for their relationship with him?

4. What do these descriptions of Old Testament anointings tell you about who God is, what he is like, and how he feels about his children?

Prayer: *Dear God, you have marked me with a seal—an anointing that cannot be taken away. Just as you cared for the Israelites, you care for me today. Anoint me, Father, with the oil of gladness. Cover me in your grace and mercy. Thank you for giving me these good and holy things. May I remember my anointing. As others try to discourage me, may I know that nothing can separate me from your love. As circumstances start to weigh me down, may I remember that I am anointed with gladness. In Jesus' name I pray, amen.*

3 The Anointing of Christ

Jesus himself was anointed. You read one story about his anointing in session 3, when the Holy Spirit descended on him in the form of a dove (see Matthew 3:16). But Jesus was also once anointed by an unlikely source. Read the following story from Luke's Gospel:

> **Luke 7:36–39, 44–47:** *When one of the Pharisees invited Jesus to have dinner with him, he went to the Pharisee's house and reclined at the table. A woman in that town who*

*lived a sinful life learned that Jesus was eating at the Phari-
see's house, so she came there with an alabaster jar of perfume. As she stood behind him at his feet weeping, she began
to wet his feet with her tears. Then she wiped them with her
hair, kissed them and poured perfume on them.*

*When the Pharisee who had invited him saw this, he
said to himself, "If this man were a prophet, he would know
who is touching him and what kind of woman she is—that
she is a sinner." . . .*

*Then he turned toward the woman and said to Simon,
"Do you see this woman? I came into your house. You did
not give me any water for my feet, but she wet my feet with
her tears and wiped them with her hair. You did not give me
a kiss, but this woman, from the time I entered, has not
stopped kissing my feet. You did not put oil on my head, but
she has poured perfume on my feet. Therefore, I tell you, her
many sins have been forgiven—as her great love has shown.
But whoever has been forgiven little loves little."*

1. When you think about anointing ceremonies, what type
   of people come to mind as the ones performing the anointing? Why do these people come to mind?

2. How do the woman's actions in this passage mimic an anointing ceremony?

3. What does it say about Jesus that he allowed a woman "who lived a sinful life" to anoint him? How do you think this anointing impacted him?

4. Where do you see yourself in this story: as a Pharisee judging the woman's actions, as Jesus being the willing participant, or as the sinful woman, kissing Jesus' feet? Why?

Prayer: *God, you are a good father who loves all of his children, no matter how great their sin. Because of your Son, I am accepted in this upside-down kingdom where the last are first and the first are last, where the meek are blessed, and where the poor in spirit are cared for. Thank you for sending Jesus as an example of one who accepted and loved all—one who broke societal norms to prove the greatness of your love. May I feel, know, and believe the greatness of your love toward me. May I be overwhelmed by this love and filled with gratitude like the woman in this story, falling at Jesus' feet in response. In his name I pray, amen.*

4 Your Anointing

Anointing did not end in the Old Testament, nor did it end with Jesus. If you are in Christ, you are also anointed. You are covered by God's grace, mercy, and love. Even if you have not been *literally* anointed by oil, you can rest assured that the Spirit covers you fully and completely. Read what the Bible has to say about your anointing after Jesus ascended to heaven:

Acts 2:14–18: *Then Peter stood up with the Eleven, raised his voice and addressed the crowd: "Fellow Jews and all of you who live in Jerusalem, let me explain this to you; listen carefully to what I say. These people are not drunk, as you suppose. It's only nine in the morning! No, this is what was spoken by the prophet Joel: 'In the last days, God says, I will pour out my Spirit on all people. Your sons and daughters will prophesy, your young men will see visions, your old men will dream dreams Even on my servants, both men and women, I will pour out my Spirit in those days, and they will prophesy.' "*

2 Corinthians 1:21–22: *Now it is God who makes both us and you stand firm in Christ. He anointed us, set his seal of ownership on us, and put his Spirit in our hearts as a deposit, guaranteeing what is to come.*

1 John 2:24–27: *As for you, see that what you have heard from the beginning remains in you. If it does, you also will remain in the Son and in the Father. And this is what he promised us—eternal life. I am writing these things to you about those who are trying to lead you astray. As for you, the anointing you received from him remains in you, and* *you do not need anyone to teach you. But as his anointing teaches you about all things and as that anointing is real, not counterfeit—just as it has taught you, remain in him.*

1. Do you feel like you've been anointed by the Holy Spirit? Why or why not?

2. According to these verses, what does your anointing allow you to do? What assurances does it provide to you?

3. The 1 John 2:24–27 passage emphasizes the idea of remaining in Christ. How do you remain in Christ? How does the Spirit help you to do so?

4. These passages tell us the Holy Spirit has been poured out over our lives. How could this truth change the way you approach your day?

Prayer: *Pick one of the passages from today's study. What truth do you need the most? The promise in Acts 2 that the Holy Spirit allows you to prophesy—or have discernment—in your circumstances? The promise in 2 Corinthians that Christ anointed you with his seal of ownership and you belong to him? Or the promise in 1 John that says no one can lead you astray when we have been anointed by the Spirit? Whatever truth you need most today, meditate on that passage for a few moments as your prayer time. Ask God to give you what is promised. Ask him to help you believe that you have already received these promises.*

For Next Session: *Write down any insights or questions you want to discuss at the next group meeting. In preparation for the next session, read chapters 8, 12, and 13 in* Help Is Here.

Our Gift-Giver
of Life

The written law brings death, but the Spirit gives life.

2 CORINTHIANS 3:6 NCV

Welcome

I f you were never selected for the "gifted and talented" class at your school, or you never received the MVP award, or you never landed the lead in the play, it might be hard to consider yourself a *gifted* person. In our society, gifted people are the ones who win the races, ace the tests, and get the prize at the singing contests. The rest of us are just . . . well, *us*.

But this is not how God sees you! As you will discover in this week's final session, at the moment of your conversion, the Holy Spirit gifted you with gifts. These gifts may not turn heads in the secular world, but they do in the spiritual realm. Paul listed some of these gifts in his first letter to the Corinthians: "To one there is given through the Spirit a message of wisdom, to another a message of knowledge by means of the same Spirit, to another faith by the same Spirit, to another gifts of healing by that one Spirit" (1 Corinthians 12:8–9).

The gifts of the Spirit are different from earthly gifts or talents in several ways. First, they are *free*. No work, practice, or earning is necessary to receive them. Second, they are all equally *important*. You aren't given first, second, or third place for your spiritual gifts. As Paul also wrote, "There are diversities of gifts, but the same Spirit. There are differences of ministries, but the same Lord" (1 Corinthians 12:4–5 NKJV). Furthermore, you have been given the gifts of the Spirit not only for your own benefit but also for the benefit of those around you. The gifts that you have spill out to others—blessing them, encouraging them, and healing them.

If you're skeptical that you could have such a significant impact on others, remember that it is the Holy Spirit at work within you that allows your gifts to be poured out onto others—just as he has been poured out onto you. So, as you work through this final session, may you feel empowered by the gifts the Holy Spirit has given to you and confident that when you share them with others, their lives will be changed in the way the Spirit has changed yours.

Share

Welcome to session five of the *Help Is Here* study. To get things started for this week's final group time, discuss one of the following questions:

- What is your "history" with spiritual gifts? Did your religious upbringing focus on them, dismiss them, ignore them? Explain your answer.

— or —

- What is the most memorable thing you've learned about the Holy Spirit in this study so far? Why was that memorable to you?

Read

Break into groups of two to three people one last time to read through the following passage from the Gospel of Matthew, and then take a few minutes to write down your responses to the questions that follow. Share your answers with each other before you rejoin the main group.

"I baptize you with water for repentance. But after me comes one who is more powerful than I, whose sandals I am not worthy to carry. He will baptize you with the Holy Spirit and fire. His winnowing fork is in his hand, and he will clear his threshing floor, gathering his wheat into the barn and burning up the chaff with unquenchable fire."

Matthew 3:11–12

- John the Baptist spoke these words to describe the type of baptism that he was doing. But what does he say about the type of baptism that the "more powerful" one will do?

- What do you think it means to baptize with both the "Holy Spirit and fire"?

Watch

Now watch the video for this session. Fill in the blanks below as you follow along with the teaching and record any thoughts or ideas that stand out to you.

1. The Holy Spirit is the ultimate _____ from God. A gift he gave to empower you, guide you, bring you peace, intercede and advocate for you. But the Holy Spirit is also the ultimate gift-_____ .

2. A soul baptized in the Spirit is a soul that is _____. Just like fire, the Holy Spirit will not be quenched as long as we provide _____ for him to do his work.

3. The book of Acts reveals the Holy Spirit to be the ultimate gift-giver. He garnished the _____ with supernatural abilities that glorified God, blessed the needy, and edified the _____ .

4. When you look at Paul's words in 1 Corinthians 12:8–11, you find the gifts fit into categories:

Category 1: Discerning Gifts

- A word of _____ is a message rightly suited for the occasion.

- A word of _____ is a gift of information that a person has no way of knowing apart from the Holy Spirit.

- Discerning of _____ is an ability to identify and fight against evil spirits.

Category 2: Dynamic Gifts

- To have the gift of _____ is to enjoy a sense of super-natural, contagious confidence.

- Gifts of _____ include the choice of the Holy Spirit to render restoration though the prayers of a saint.

- Working of _____ happens when God chooses to alter a person's circumstances.

Category 3: Declarative Gifts

- To _____ is to build up and encourage.

- Speaking in _____ and the interpretation of _____ are as magnificent as they are controversial. The gift of tongues was actually on display on the Day of Pentecost.

5. When the Paul used the phrase " _____ of the Spirit," he almost always used the Greek term *charisma* or *charismata*. A *charisma* is a _____ in the purest sense of the word.

6. Jesus gave his _____ as he had given himself on the cross. As a gift, _____ and undeserved.

Discuss

Take some time to discuss what you just watched by answering the following questions.

1. How is the Holy Spirit like fire?

2. Read Acts 2:1–13. How would you describe what happened in this scene?

3. Have you ever been a part of a gathering where the Holy Spirit was clearly at work like he was in this passage? If so, what was that experience like for you?

4. Read 1 Corinthians 12:4–11. Which spiritual gift, or gifts, do you think you have? Why?

5. Do you consider some spiritual gifts more important than others? If so, which ones?

6. What is one way you could serve someone else using your spiritual gifts this week?

Respond

On your own, write down the names of everyone in your group. Beside his or her name, list a gift, or gifts, that you have seen in that person. It can be one of the spiritual gifts Paul listed in 1 Corinthians 12:8–10, or another gift you've seen this individual exhibit. When you're finished writing, and if you have time, share what you've written with each member of the group.

Name: _____   Gift(s): _____

Name: _____   Gift(s): _____

Name: _____   Gift(s): _____

Name: _____   Gift(s): _____

Name: _____   Gift(s): _____

Name: _____   Gift(s): _____

Name: _____   Gift(s): _____

Name: _____   Gift(s): _____

Name: _____   Gift(s): _____

Pray

End your time by leading your group in prayer, or pray the following prayer aloud together:

Father, we thank you for this time together we've had as a group. Thank you, Spirit, for guiding us, for teaching us about you, for speaking to us in big and small ways. May we continue to learn about you and feel your presence. May you be poured over us each day in power, and may we feel encouraged and emboldened by the truth that because of Jesus' sacrifice, God is always with us in the form of his Spirit. In Jesus' name we pray, amen.

Ask if anyone has any prayer requests or answers to prayer to share. Write any requests down in the space below so you can continue to pray for those needs in the weeks ahead.

Name   Request

_____   _____

_____   _____

_____   _____

_____   _____

_____   _____

_____   _____

WATCH ANSWERS: (1) GIFT, GIVER; (2) ABLAZE, FUEL; (3) BELIEVERS, CHURCH; (4) CATEGORY 1: WISDOM, KNOWLEDGE, SPIRITS; CATEGORY 2: FAITH, HEALING, MIRACLES; CATEGORY 3: PROPHESY, TONGUES, TONGUES; (5) GIFTS, GIFT; (6) SPIRIT, PURE

Personal Study

God's intended rescue center for this hurting world is the church. As members of the body of Christ, we are to provide a haven for hurting people, a safe place to come in out of the storm. We each have responsibilities, and when we work together, the displaced find a place. Behind it all is the Holy Spirit—and he oversees it all through the distribution of spiritual gifts.

1 The Holy Spirit as Fire

•••

So far in this study, you've learned about a few different metaphors used to describe the Holy Spirit: the Holy Spirit as a dove, the Holy Spirit as a helper, the Holy Spirit as a guide, and the Holy Spirit as a mother. This week, you learned about the Holy Spirit as fire. The Spirit is like fire in a few different ways. First, the Spirit is a refining fire, ridding us of our sin and impurities. Second, the Spirit is like a fire that melts away our hard-heartedness, doubt, and fear. Third, the

Spirit is like fire in that it burns within us, filling us with hope, passion, and purpose. Because of this, we are warned in Scripture to not put out the flame, but to it keep it going with a steady faith. Read the following verses that compare the Holy Spirit to fire:

Matthew 3:11–12: *"I baptize you with water for repentance. But after me comes one who is more powerful than I, whose sandals I am not worthy to carry. He will baptize you with the Holy Spirit and fire. His winnowing fork is in his hand, and he will clear his threshing floor, gathering his wheat into the barn and burning up the chaff with unquenchable fire."*

Acts 2:1–4: *When the day of Pentecost came, they were all together in one place. Suddenly a sound like the blowing of a violent wind came from heaven and filled the whole house where they were sitting. They saw what seemed to be tongues of fire that separated and came to rest on each of them. All of them were filled with the Holy Spirit and began to speak in other tongues as the Spirit enabled them.*

1 Thessalonians 5:19–22: *Do not quench the Spirit. Do not treat prophecies with contempt but test them all; hold on to what is good, reject every kind of evil.*

1. Which metaphor for the Holy Spirit that you've learned about in this study has been the most interesting or helpful for you? Why?

2. In Matthew 3:11–12, Jesus says that he will baptize us in fire. What does this mean? Have you ever experienced Jesus' refining fire?

3. In Acts 2:14, the Holy Spirit could have simply given the crowd at Pentecost the ability to speak and understand different languages, but he chose to visually reveal himself in the form of small flames above the believers' heads. Why do you think the Spirit showed up in this way and in the form of fire?

4. In 1 Thessalonians 5:19, Paul warns against quenching the Holy Spirit. Do you feel the Spirit is alive in you today, or is it quenched? How do you know?

Prayer: *Holy Spirit, come alive in me today. I confess that I can go days, months, and entire seasons without acknowledging your presence in my life. I do not want to quench your fire! I want it to grow. Make me aware of your power and your ability in my life. Remind me to call on you when I need help rather than relying on myself. Fan the flame of my faith. May it rise high so that others can see it inside me. In Jesus' name I pray, amen.*

2 All Gifts Are Created Equal
• • •

It's counter-cultural to believe the gifts of the Spirit are equal in God's eyes. As humans, we are constantly sizing each other up, trying to decide who is the fastest, smartest, or prettiest. As Christians, this is also a temptation. We look around our church and think that some people are more spiritual than others based on their spiritual gifts. The preacher can teach and reveal truths from the Bible—that person must be more spiritual. Another serves day in and day out—that person must be more spiritual. But Paul warns against this type of comparison. Read the following passage about spiritual gifts and their importance in the body of Christ:

> **1 Corinthians 12:4–6, 12–20:** *There are different kinds of gifts, but the same Spirit distributes them. There are different kinds of service, but the same Lord. There are different kinds of working, but in all of them and in everyone it is the same God at work. . . .*
>
> *Just as a body, though one, has many parts, but all its many parts forms one body, so it is with Christ. For we were all baptized by one Spirit so as to form one body—whether Jews or Gentiles, slave or free—and we were all given the one Spirit to drink. Even so the body is not made up of one part but of many.*
>
> *Now if the foot should say, "Because I am not a hand, I do not belong to the body," it would not for that reason stop being part of the body. And if the ear should say, "Because I am not an eye, I do not belong to the body," it would not for that reason stop being part of the body. If the whole body were an eye, where would the sense of hearing be? If the*

whole body were an ear, where would the sense of smell be? But in fact God has placed the parts in the body, every one of them, just as he wanted them to be. If they were all one part, where would the body be? As it is, there are many parts, but one body.

1. What spiritual gifts have you viewed as most important and least important? Why?

2. Underline every word in this passage that suggests unity, such as *one* and *all.* What does this tell you about how we are all supposed to behave as followers of Christ?

3. How does considering one gift more important than another weaken the body of Christ? Have you ever seen this happen in your faith community? If so, how?

4. Think about God's ideal church. What would it look like? How would we as believers behave toward each other and ourselves?

Prayer: *Dear God, I confess I often bring the ways of this world into your church. I compare myself to others. I belittle my own gifts and uplift others'. Or I think of myself as more important than others based on my abilities. Humble me, God. Allow me to see the body of Christ as united by your grace and the blood of Jesus. Strengthen my faith community and protect us from comparison. May we focus on you—and you alone—and be united by your truth. I pray this in the name of Jesus and by the power of the Holy Spirit. Amen.*

3 What Is Your Gift?

Spend some time today deciphering what your spiritual gift, or gifts, might be. Perhaps you already know. Perhaps you have no idea. Or maybe your spiritual gifting has changed over the years as you've changed as a person. Read the list of gifts Paul gives in 1 Corinthians below:

Discerning Gifts: *To one is given the word of wisdom through the Spirit, to another the word of knowledge . . . to another discerning of spirits* (1 Corinthians 12:8, 10 NKJV).

Dynamic Gifts: *To another faith by the same Spirit, to another gifts of healings by the same Spirit, to another the working of miracles* (1 Corinthians 12:9–10 NKJV).

Declarative Gifts: *To another prophecy . . . to another different kinds of tongues, to another the interpretation of tongues* (1 Corinthians 12:10 NKJV).

1. What gifts and talents do you have—whether those are specific spiritual gifts you're aware of or general gifts you've seen in yourself and that others have seen in you?

2. According to the gifts listed in this passage, which ones do you think you have? How have you seen these gifts play out in your life?

3. Of the gifts you don't have, who are some people you know who do have them? How can you tell they have these gifts?

4. Do you feel that you are using your spiritual gifts, whether at your church, at work, or in your community? If so, how? If not, why not?

Prayer: *Lord, give me a vision today for what using my spiritual gifts could look like, whether at my church or in my community. Please reveal how I can use my gifts to bless others and help me overcome obstacles that keep me from using my gifts. In Jesus' name, amen.*

4 The Free Gift of the Spirit

When Paul wrote about the gifts of the Spirit, he used the Greek word *charisma* or *charismata*. This word indicates a gift in the purest sense of the word—something we receive but don't deserve. This is the best part about the gifts of the Spirit: we don't have to earn them. By God's grace, they are simply bestowed on us. The same is true of the Spirit. He is not something we earn once we've achieved a certain status of spirituality. He is something we receive into our lives when we become followers of Jesus. Read the following passage from the Gospel of John about how Jesus gifted the disciples with his Spirit:

> **John 20:19–22:** *On the evening of that first day of the week, when the disciples were together, with the doors locked for fear of the Jewish leaders, Jesus came and stood among*

them and said, "Peace be with you!" After he said this, he showed them his hands and side. The disciples were overjoyed when they saw the Lord. Again Jesus said, "Peace be with you! As the Father has sent me, I am sending you." And with that he breathed on them and said, "Receive the Holy Spirit."

1. At the beginning of this study, would you say you had received the Holy Spirit in your life? Why or why not? What would you say now?

2. Put yourself in this moment. Jesus had just died, and the disciples were worried about the authorities and questioning what to do next. How do you think they felt when they saw Jesus? What do you think they felt when Jesus breathed his Spirit onto them?

3. What action was required of the disciples in order to receive the Spirit? What does this tell you about how Christ bestows his Spirit on us?

4. Have you had an encounter with Jesus or the Holy Spirit like this? If so, describe that experience. If not, what kind of encounter with Christ or the Spirit do you need today?

Prayer: *Father, thank you for this opportunity to learn more about you, your Son, and your Spirit. May I carry these lessons with me today and every day. May I remember that I have done nothing to earn the Holy Spirit's presence in my life—but I have it nonetheless. Your nearness and power are a gift to me made possible by the sacrifice of Jesus. May I cling to this gift when times get hard, when I am questioning my own worth, and when I am questioning you. May I hear, feel, and sense the Holy Spirit beside me and inside me, speaking words of love, and grace, and guidance. Thank you for this most precious gift. In your name I pray, amen.*

Leader's Guide

T hank you for your willingness to lead your group through this study! What you have chosen to do is valuable and will make a great difference in the lives of others. The rewards of being a leader are different from those of participating, and we hope that as you lead you will find your own journey with Christ deepened by this experience.

Help Is Here is a five-session Bible study built around video content and small-group interaction. As the group leader, imagine yourself as the host of a party. Your job is to take care of your guests by managing the behind-the-scenes details so that when your guests arrive, they can focus on one another and on the interaction around the topic for that session.

Your role as group leader is not to answer all the questions or reteach the content—the video, book, and study guide will do most of that work. Your job is to guide the experience and cultivate your group into a connected and engaged community. This will make it a place for members to process, question, and reflect—not necessarily receive more instruction.

There are several elements in this leader's guide that will help you as you structure your study and reflection time, so be sure to follow along and take advantage of each one.

Before You Begin

Before your first meeting, make sure the group members have a copy of this study guide. Alternatively, you can hand out the study guides at your first meeting and give the members some time to look over the material and ask any preliminary questions. Also make sure they are aware that they have access to the streaming videos at any time by following the instructions printed on the inside front cover. During your first meeting, ask the members to provide their name, phone number, and email address so you can keep in touch with them.

Generally, the ideal size for a group is eight to ten people, which will ensure that everyone has enough time to participate in discussions. If you have more people, you might want to break up the main group into smaller subgroups. Encourage those who show up at the first meeting to commit to attending the duration of the study, as this will help the group members get to know one another, create stability for the group, and help you know how to best prepare to lead them through the material.

Each of the sessions begins with an opening reflection in the "Welcome" section. The questions that follow in the "Share" section serve as an icebreaker to get the group members thinking about the topic at hand. Some people may want to tell a long story in response to one of these questions, but the goal is to keep the answers brief. Ideally, you want everyone in the group to get a chance to answer, so try to keep the responses to a minute or less. If you have talkative group members, say up front that everyone needs to limit their answer to one minute.

Give the group members a chance to answer, but also tell them to feel free to pass if they wish. With the rest of the study, it's generally not a good idea to have everyone answer every question—a free-flowing discussion is more desirable. But with the opening icebreaker questions, you can go around the circle. Encourage shy people to share, but don't force them.

At your first meeting, let the group members know that each session contains a personal study section they can use to continue to engage with the content until the next meeting. While this is an optional exercise, it will help the members cement the concepts presented during the group study time and help them better understand the character, nature, attributes, and role of Holy Spirit by spending time in God's Word.

Let them know that if they choose to do so, they can watch the video for the next session by accessing the streaming code found on the inside front cover of their studies. Invite them to bring any questions and insights to your next meeting—especially if they had a breakthrough moment or didn't understand something.

Preparation for Each Session

As the leader, there are a few things you should do to prepare for each meeting:

- **Read through the session.** This will help you to become more familiar with the content and know how to structure the discussion times.

- **Decide how the videos will be used.** Determine whether you want the members to watch the videos ahead of time (via the streaming access code found on the inside front cover) or together as a group.

- **Decide which questions you want to discuss.** Based on the length of group discussion, you may not be able to get through all the questions, so choose four to five that you definitely want to cover.

- **Be familiar with questions you want to discuss.** When the group meets, you will be watching the clock, so you want to make sure you are familiar with the questions you have selected. In this way, you'll ensure you have the material more deeply in your mind than your group members.

- **Pray for your group.** Pray for your group and ask God to lead them as they study his Word.

In many cases, there will be no one "right" answer to the question. Answers will vary, especially when the group members are being asked to share their personal experiences.

Structuring the Discussion Time

You will need to determine with your group how long you want to meet so you can plan your time accordingly. Generally, most groups like to meet for either ninety minutes or two hours, so you could use one of the following schedules:

SECTION	90 MIN.	120 MIN.
WELCOME (members arrive and get settled)	10 minutes	15 minutes
SHARE (discuss one or more of the opening questions for the session)	10 minutes	15 minutes
READ (discuss the questions based on the Scripture reading for the session)	10 minutes	15 minutes
WATCH (watch the teaching material together and take notes)	20 minutes	20 minutes
DISCUSS (discuss the Bible study questions that you selected ahead of time)	30 minutes	40 minutes
RESPOND & PRAY (pray together as a group and dismiss)	10 minutes	15 minutes

As the group leader, it is up to you to keep track of the time and keep things on schedule. You might want to set a timer for each segment so both you and the group members know when your time is up. (There are some good phone apps for timers that play a gentle chime or other pleasant sound instead of a disruptive noise.)

Don't be concerned if the group members are quiet or slow to share. People are often quiet when they are pulling together their ideas, and this might be a new experience for them. Just ask a question and let it hang in the air until someone shares. You can then say, "Thank you. What about others? What came to you when you watched that portion of the teaching?"

Group Dynamics

Leading a group through *Help Is Here* will be rewarding to you and your group members. But you still may encounter challenges! Discussions can get off track. Group members may not be sensitive to the needs and ideas of others. Some might worry they will be expected to talk about matters that make them feel awkward. Others may express comments that result in disagreements. To help ease this strain on you and the group, consider the following ground rules:

- When someone raises a question or comment that is off the main topic, suggest that you deal with it another time, or, if you feel led to go in that direction, let the group know you will be spending some time discussing it.

- If someone asks a question that you don't know how to answer, admit it and move on. At your discretion, feel free to invite group members to comment on questions that call for personal experience.

- If you find one or two people are dominating the discussion time, direct a few questions to others in the group. Outside the main group time, ask the more dominating members to help you draw out the quieter ones. Work to make them a part of the solution instead of part of the problem.

- When a disagreement occurs, encourage the group members to process the matter in love. Encourage

those on opposite sides to restate what they heard
the other side say about the matter, and then invite
each side to evaluate if that perception is accurate.
Lead the group in examining other Scriptures related to the topic and look for common ground.

When any of these issues arise, encourage your group
members to follow these words from the Bible: "Love one
another" (John 13:34), "If it is possible, as far as it depends
on you, live at peace with everyone" (Romans 12:18), "Whatever is true . . . noble . . . right . . . if anything is excellent or
praiseworthy—think about such things" (Philippians 4:8),
and, "Be quick to listen, slow to speak and slow to become
angry" (James 1:19). This will make your group time more
rewarding and beneficial for everyone who attends.

Thank you again for taking the time to lead your group.
You are making a difference in the lives of others and hav-
ing an impact on their journey toward understanding the
Holy Spirit.

ALSO AVAILABLE FROM
MAX LUCADO

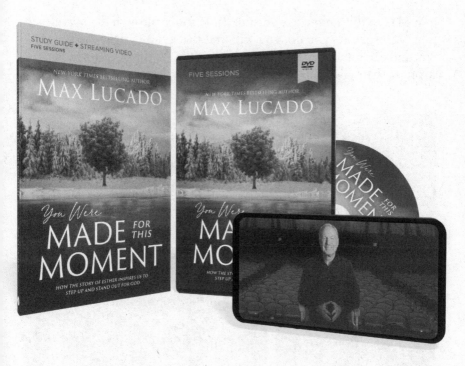

Study Guide plus Streaming Video
9780310136255

DVD
9780310136279

Available now at your favorite bookstore,
or streaming video on StudyGateway.com.

GOD IS NEARER THAN YOU KNOW

In *You Are Never Alone*, Max Lucado reminds us that God's presence and power are nearer than we think. We need only look to the miracles of Jesus as told in the Gospel of John to know this is true.

Join Max in this unique six-session Bible study through the miracles in John's Gospel. As you do, you will find that Jesus is right there with you and cares about every aspect of your life. You will realize you are stronger than you think because God is nearer than you know.

Study Guide
9780310115557

DVD with Free Streaming
9780310115571

Available now at your favorite bookstore,
or streaming video on StudyGateway.com.

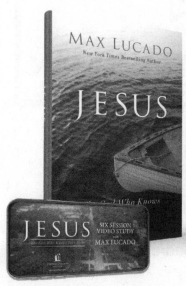
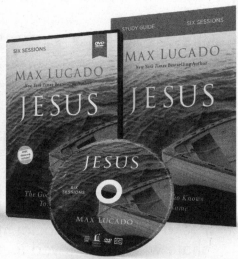